P9-AZW-386

AWESOME JOKES

7

THAT EVERY

YEAR OLD

SHOULD

KNOW!

Copyright © 2018 by Say So Media Ltd.

All rights reserved.

No part of this book may be reproduced in any form or by any
electronic or mechanical means including information storage and
retrieval systems, without permission in writing from the author.

Names, characters, places, and products are used fictitiously. Any resemblance to
actual persons, living or dead, events, or locales is entirely coincidental. If you can't
make your parents laugh with these jokes, maybe you need new parents?

Depending on where you live, some spellings might seem odd to you like colour,
or favourite. I've done it on purpose: I'm aktually quite good at spelling. OK, it's
because I'm from England and I'm no good at baseball jokes. Just skip over the ones
you don't understand, and I hope you enjoy the others!

Additional research: Olivera Ristovska

Design: Fanni Williams / thehappycolourstudio.com
Icons made by: Freepik from www.flaticon.com

www.matwaugh.co.uk

Produced by Big Red Button Books,
a division of Say So Media Ltd.

ISBN: 978-1-9999147-3-8

Published: March 2018
This edition: July 2019

AWESOME JOKES

7 THAT EVERY YEAR OLD SHOULD KNOW!

MAT WAUGH
ILLUSTRATIONS BY INDREK SILVER EINBERG

Introduction

What makes you laugh?

I saw a video of a dog on a skateboard. That made me chuckle.

My brother once lost his welly in the mud. That made me laugh out loud.

My friend once told me a joke that was so funny, it actually made me cry. It's in this book (but you'll have to find it yourself).

This book is full of all the best jokes I know. Use them to find out which grown-ups are fun, and which ones are probably dead.

Or just tell them to your friends. I did!

PS Know a better one? Get it on the Awesome Map! See the back pages.

Let's Get Cracking!

What's less scary than finding a tiger at your front door?
Discovering a dandelion in your garden!

How long will my spaghetti be?
About 30 centimetres, madam.

What's a butcher's favourite pet?
A sausage dog!

 **I used to like tractors, but I don't any more. I'm an ex-tractor fan.**

Where do cows go on holiday?
Moo York!

 **I just swallowed a bone.**
Are you choking?
No, I really did!

Knock Knock! Who's there?
Dishes!
Dishes who?
Dishes definitely the worst joke in this book.

What do you get when you cross a bear with a freezer?

A teddy brrrr!

 **I can see into the future!**
How odd. When did this start?
Next Friday.

There are two types of people in this world: People who love ice cream and people who don't tell the truth.

What happened to the spirit who got too close to the fire?

He turned into a toasty ghostie!

What should you offer a hungry cannibal?

Give him a hand!

How do you catch a squirrel?
Climb a tree and pretend to be nuts!

 **I think I'm turning into an orange. Is there anything I can do?**
Have you tried playing squash?

What kind of hair do oceans have?

Wavy!

I've swallowed my pocket money!
Take this tablet and we'll see if there's any change in the morning.

 **I have a ringing in my ears.**
Yes, sorry about that. I forgot to turn my phone off.

Why did the boy push his bed into the fireplace?
Because he wanted to sleep like a log!

 **My bowl's wet!**
That's not wet, madam - that's the soup!

 **My brother here keeps thinking he's invisible!**
What brother?

Where do burgers go to dance?
To the meat-ball!

Where do astronauts keep their sandwiches?
In their launch boxes.

 **What do cannibals have for lunch?**
Baked beings!

Why did the strawberry cry?
Because all his friends were in a jam!

Who turns the lights off at Halloween?

The light's witch!

How do astronauts drink their tea?
From flying saucers!

Knock Knock!

Who's there?
Avenue.
Avenue who?
Avenue knocked on my door before?

What's the smartest insect?
A spelling bee.

What is a monkey's favourite cookie?
Chocolate chimp!

Knock Knock!

Who's there?
Icy!
Icy who?
Icy a giant polar behind you!

The bottom of the butter
bucket is the buttered
bucket bottom.

TONGUE
TWISTER

DOCTOR,
DOCTOR!

I woke up with an insect dancing
on my nose.
Don't worry, it's just a bug that's
going around!

What did the
painter say to
the wall?

Don't worry,
I've got you
covered

Knock Knock!

Who's there?
Cook.
Cook who?
You're definitely cuckoo. In fact I'd say you're crazy.

What's a ghost's favourite Christmas entertainment?

A phantomime!

What did one plate say to the other?
The dinner's on me!

Knock Knock!

Who's there?
Witch.
Witch who?
Witch one of you left your broomstick in the porch?

DOCTOR, DOCTOR! **What can I do about my broken leg?**
Limp.

Knock Knock!
Who's there?
Aries!
Aries who?
Aries a good reason why I talk this way.
Let me in and I'll explain!

What did the angry Italian waiter give the customer?
A pizza his mind!

Knock Knock!

Who's there?
Mickey.
Mickey who?
Mickey won't fit, that's why I knocked.

I'm worried about the size of my waste.
Nonsense – you're talking rubbish!

What is a tree's favourite drink?

Root beer!

 Knock Knock!

Who's there?
Emma.
Emma who?
Emma bit cold here, can you let me in?

How do monsters tell their future?
They read a horror-scope.

 **Why were the trick-or-treaters wearing grass skirts?**
Because it was Hulaween!

Who's there?
Bass!
Bass who?
Bass the car keys through the letterbox please, I forgot them!

What do you call a fly with a sore throat?

A hoarse fly!

Why do pandas like old films?
Because they're black and white.

DOCTOR, DOCTOR!

You said I'd be dead in ten. But ten what? Years? Months?
10, 9, 8, 7, 6...

I have a dog that does magic tricks. He's a labra-cadabra-dor!

Who's there?
Heaven.
Heaven who?
Heaven seen you in ages!

What did the ice cream say to the unhappy cake?
Hey, what's eating you?

DOCTOR, DOCTOR! ➕

What can you give me to stop my hair falling out?
How about a shower cap?

Why did Mickey Mouse go into space?
He was looking for Pluto.

Knock Knock!

Who's there?
Tad!
Tad who?
Tad's all folks!

What has one eye but can't see?
A needle!

Why did the fruit punch and the cereal box?

Because they were having a food fight!

 **What makes music in your hair?**
A head band!

 **Who's there?**
Lego!
Lego who?
Lego of my arm and I'll tell you!

How do you stop a child from moaning in the back seat of a car?
Put him in the front seat.

How do you make a goldfish old?
Take away his G!

Can you smell
carrots?

What did the snowman say to his friend?
Can you smell carrots?

What did the grape do when it was crushed?
It let out a little whine.

What's the easiest way to find a princess?
Follow the foot Prince.

Knock Knock!

Who's there?
Jamaican.
Jamaican who?
Jamaican me crazy!

DOCTOR, DOCTOR!

I keep thinking there are two of me.
One at a time please!

What colour socks do bears wear?

They don't wear socks, silly, they have bear feet!

Why did the chocolate go to school?
Because he wanted to be a Smartie.

Knock Knock!

Who's there?
Candice!
Candice who?
Candice joke book get any better?

I wish to wish the wish you wish to wish, but if you wish the wish the witch wishes, I won't wish the wish you wish to wish.

TONGUE TWISTER

What do you call a space magician?
A flying sorcerer!

What is a forum?

Two-um plus two-um

When does a whiny caveman eat breakfast?
In the moaning!

Everyone keeps ignoring me.
Next please!

Who's there?
Tiss.
Tiss who?
Tiss who is good for blowing
your nose.

Who's there?
Wilma!
Wilma who?
Wilma leg fall off?

Why did the man take a pencil to bed?
Because he wanted to draw the curtains!

DOCTOR, DOCTOR! ✚

I feel like a billiard ball.
Please get to the end of the queue.

Why did the sun go to school?
To get brighter!

Why don't honest people need beds?

Because they never lie.

What did the light bulb say to its mother?

I wuv you watts and watts!

What do you call a dinosaur with one eye?
A Do-you-think-he-saw-us!

82 dogs have escaped from a nearby kennels. Police say they have no leads.

Do you sell invisible ink?
Certainly madam. What colour would you like?

Knock Knock!

Who's there?
Ivor.
Ivor who?
I've a sore hand from all this knocking!

Knock Knock!

Who's there?
Barbie.
Barbie who?
Barbie-q-chicken!

**Six thick thistle sticks.
Six thick thistles stick.**

TONGUE TWISTER

If an apple comes from an apple tree and an acorn comes from an oak tree, where does a chicken come from?
A poul-tree!

DOCTOR, DOCTOR! ➕ **It hurts when I press with my finger here… and here… and here… What is the matter with me?**
You have a broken finger!

Who's there?
Dish!
Dish who?
Dish ish a shtick-up!

What did the letter say the stamp?

Stick with me and we'll go places!

Knock Knock!

Who's there?
Will.
Will who?
Will you just open the door?

Knock Knock!

Who's there?
A herd.
A herd who?
A herd you were home, so I came round to play!

What does an Eskimo like on his nachos?
Chilli sauce of course!

DOCTOR, DOCTOR!

I think I'm a pack of cards!
Hmm. I'll deal with you later.

Knock Knock!

Who's there?
Rabbit.
Rabbit who?
Rabbit up carefully –
it's a present!

Why was the broom late?
It over swept!

 **Why did the anemone blush?**
Because the sea weed!

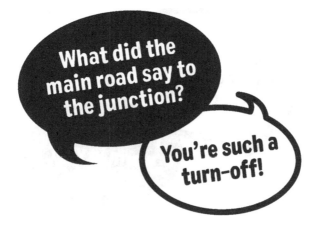

 **Some days I feel like a teepee and other days I feel like a wigwam.**
You're definitely too tents.

What do you call a cow that eats your grass?
A lawn moo-er.

What did Mars say to Saturn?
Why don't you give me a ring sometime?

What is worse than finding a worm in your apple?

Finding half a worm in your apple!

Why did the American visitor to London get run over?
Because he didn't know what the pavement!

I snore so loud I keep myself awake!
Have you tried sleeping in another room?

What kind of cats like to go bowling?
Alley cats!

What did 0 say to 8?

Nice belt!

Waiter! Waiter! There's a fly in my soup!
Don't worry madam! That spider hiding under your bread
roll will eat him soon.

What is brown and sticky?
A stick!

 **Who is always the smallest mother
at the birthday party?**
The minimum!

Knock Knock!

Who's there?
Police!
Police who?
Police hurry up, I've forgotten my coat!

DOCTOR, DOCTOR! ➕

I think I'm turning invisible!
I'm sorry, I can't see you today.

Why does Waldo wear stripes?

Because he doesn't want to be spotted!

What type of coat
do you put on
when it's wet?
A coat of paint!

Waiter, Waiter!

Can I have the bill please.
Certainly sir. How did you find
your lunch?
With a magnifying glass.

**How do you know if there's an
elephant in your refrigerator?**
Look for footprints in the butter!

**What did the pen say to the pencil
who wouldn't stop talking?**
So, what's your point?

Knock Knock!

Who's there?
Agatha!
Agatha who?
Agatha headache. Do you have
any tablets?

**What kind of driver never gets a
parking ticket?**
A screw driver!

What do you call a pig that can do karate?
A pork chop!

Knock Knock!

Who's there?
Waiter!
Waiter who?
Waiter minute while I check if I've got the right address...

How do artists protect their castle?
With a drawbridge.

 **Who's there?**
Doris.
Doris who?
Doris locked! Please let me in!

What do you get when you cross a snowman with a vampire?
Frostbite!

What did the tree say to the wind?

Leaf me alone!

Why is there a fly in my ice-cream?
Perhaps he likes downhill skiing, sir.

What's the scariest thing to hear in the night?
A dinosnore!

Why do so many inventors eat lunch at their desks?
Because they love chewing over an idea.

School Doctor: Have you ever had trouble with appendicitis?
Student: Only when I tried to spell it.

Will you remember me in 60 seconds?
Yes.
Knock Knock!
Who's there?
Hey, you didn't remember me!

When does Friday come before Thursday?
In the dictionary, silly.

What do you call people who go crazy over hot chocolate?
Cocoa-Nuts.

Who's there?

Knock Knock!

Who's there?
Tinker Bell!
Tinker Bell who?
Tinker Bell is broken!

Why are snowboots useless when the sun comes out?
They melt!

 **Why did the Oreo go to the dentist?**
Because its filling had fallen out.

What is the easiest way to make a banana split?

Cut it in half, of course!

A peanut walked into a police station yesterday to claim he'd been a-salted.

 **Who's there?**
Bed!
Bed who?
Bed you can't guess who it is!

Does your sports shop stock short socks with spots?

TONGUE TWISTER

Why did the tomato turn red?

It saw the salad dressing!

Why did the boy ask his Dad for a ladder?
He wanted to go to high school.

TONGUE TWISTER **The cat catchers can't catch caught cats.**

Who's there?
Goat.
Goat who?
Goat to the door and find out.

What do fishermen say on Halloween?
Trick or Trout!

Who's there?
Goose!
Goose who?
Goose see a doctor, you don't look well!

What's the difference between a guitar and a fish?
You can't tuna fish.

**I'll have a portion of chips.
No, make that rice instead.**
I'm a waiter, sir, not a magician.

**What do you get if you cross an
elephant with a kangaroo?**
Big holes all over Australia.

What do ghosts eat for dessert?

Ice
SCREAM!

Who's there?
Closure.
Closure who?
Closure mouth while your
eating!

What kind of music do planets sing?
Neptunes!

Who's there?
Luke.
Luke who?
Luke through the keyhole and you'll find out!

One-One was a racehorse.
Two-Two was one, too.
When One-One won one race,
Two-Two won one, too.

TONGUE TWISTER

How do you ask a dinosaur round for a bite to eat?
Tea, Rex?

I moustache you a question... but I'll shave it for later.

Where do ghosts go on holiday?
Mali-boo!

What kind of umbrella does the Queen carry on a rainy day?
A wet one.

What bow can't be tied?
A rainbow!

What does Ariel like on her toast?
Mermalade!

 **Knock Knock!**

Who's there?
Yelp!
Yelp who?
Yelp me, my finger is stuck in the keyhole!

Why did you get rid of your camel?
Because he was always giving me the hump!

Fred fed Ned bread, and Ned fed Fred bread.

 **TONGUE TWISTER**

What's the first thing a hurricane does in the morning?
Puts on his windsocks!

DOCTOR, DOCTOR! ✚

I feel like biscuits!
You mean the ones you put butter on?
Yes!
Oh, you're crackers!

What do you call a 100 year old ant that loves surprises?

An ant-EEK!

Knock Knock!

Who's there?
Thayer!
Thayer who?
Thayer sorry and I won't tell your parents!

Why is a river lazy?
It never leaves its bed.

What do phones do on birthdays?
Send a SIM card!!

What is the difference between a bull and a car?
A car only has one horn.

Knock Knock!

Who's there?
Anita.
Anita who?
Anita to borrow a pencil!

What time is it when an elephant sits on your car?
Time to get a new car!

Denise sees the fleece, Denise sees the fleas. At least Denise could sneeze and feed and freeze the fleas.

TONGUE TWISTER

Why did the cow marry the horse?

He was looking for a stable relationship!

How do you know when the moon has had its tea?
When it's full.

Knock Knock!

Who's there?
Bacon.
Bacon who?
Bacon a cake for your birthday!

TONGUE TWISTER

There was a fisherman named Fisher who fished for some fish in a fissure. Till a fish with a grin, pulled the fisherman in. Now they're fishing the fissure for Fisher.

Knock Knock!

Who's there?
Vanda.
Vanda who?
Vanda you vant me to come around?

What does a cloud put on in the morning?

Thunder-wear!

What did Cinderella wear on her feet when she went for a swim?
Glass flippers!

Who designed Noah's boat?
An ark-itect!

What kind of race is never run?
A swimming race.

What type of nut has no shell?
A doughnut!

Where do orcas play music?
Orca-stras!

**Star light, star bright. First star I see tonight.
I wish I may, I wish I might.
Oh wait, it's just a satellite.**

Knock Knock!

Who's there?
Alexia.
Alexia who?
Alexia again to open this door!

Teacher: What can you tell me about the Dead Sea?
Student: Dead? I didn't even know it was sick!

What do you call it when one cat sues another?
A claw-suit.

TONGUE TWISTER

She saw Sherif's shoes on the sofa. But was she so sure she saw Sherif's shoes on the sofa?

Knock Knock!

Who's there?
Zookeeper.
Zookeeper who?
Zookeeper away from me!

What did the mum tomato say to the baby tomato?

Catch-up please!

Why did the teacher write the questions on the windows?
He wanted the lesson to be very clear!

Where do giraffes learn to read?
At High School!

What did the teacher shout when someone broke wind?
I'll get to the bottom of this!

 **What did the baby corn say to its mum?**
Where is pop corn?

**What do you call a fish
with no eyes?**
Fsh!

Why couldn't the village idiot go water-skiing?
He couldn't find a lake on a slope.

**Knock
Knock!**

Who's there?
Stopwatch.
Stopwatch who?
Stopwatch you're doing and
open this door!

**What did one firefly
say to the other?**
Got to glow now!

**Knock
Knock!**

Who's there?
Peg.
Peg who?
Peg your pardon – I've got
the wrong door.

 **Knock Knock!**

Who's there?
Eddy.
Eddy who?
Eddy idea how I can
unblock my dose?

 **Waiter, Waiter!**

**There's a grasshopper in
my soup!**
I'll tell him to hop it.

**How does an astronaut
calm a crying baby?**
Rocket to sleep!

DOCTOR, DOCTOR! ✚

I feel like a spoon.
Sit still and don't cause a stir.

**What's the only
button you can't get
fixed at a tailor's?**
Your belly button!

Doctor, Doctor! I think I need glasses.
You certainly do, sir, this is a butcher's shop!

Who's there?
Abyssinia!
Abyssinia who?
Abyssinia when I get back.

This chicken tastes rubbery!
Thank you berry much, I tell the chef!

What's at the end of everything?

G!

Why did the crayon cry?
He was feeling blue.

Why did the clown go to the doctor?
Because he was feeling a little funny!

 **Mum: Shannon, go outside and play with your whistle. I can't read my magazine.**
Shannon: Why not? I'm only seven and I can read it.

Why did the boy put chocolates under his pillow?
So he would have sweet dreams!

What kind of building has more stories than any other?

A library!

When is it bad luck to meet a black cat?
When you're a mouse.

 **I keep thinking I'm a nit.**
Why do you think that?
My wife keeps telling me to get out of her hair.

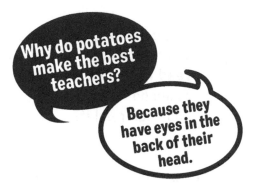

Why do potatoes make the best teachers?

Because they have eyes in the back of their head.

Daughter: I will never learn to spell.
Mum: Why not?
Daughter: The teacher keeps changing the words.

Knock Knock!

Who's there?
Scott.
Scott who?
Scott nothing to do with you!

What medicine should you give a poorly ant?
Anti-biotics.

How do penguins relax?
They chill out, of course!

What do you shout when a monkey explodes?
Baboom!

Who's there?
Sid!
Sid who?
Sid down and have a glass of juice.

A synonym for cinnamon is a cinnamon synonym

What do Mexican bears like to eat?
Bear-itos!

What do you have in December that you don't have in any other month?

D!

Why did the policeman arrest the bird of prey who flew into town with a belly ache?
For being an ill-eagle immigrant!

What do you call a dinosaur that never stops talking?
A dino-bore.

Knock Knock!

Who's there?
Butter!
Butter who?
It's butter if I don't tell you.

Knock Knock!

Who's there?
Aaron!
Aaron who?
Why Aaron you opening the door?

What's a teacher's favourite nation?
Expla-nation.

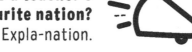

What kind of car does Mickey Mouse's wife drive?
A Minnie van!

Why couldn't the astronaut book a hotel room on the moon?
Because it was full, of course.

Where do sick wasps go?

To waspital!

What do you get when you cross a cat and a lemon?
A sourpuss!

Who's there?
Figs.
Figs who?
Figs your doorbell, it's broken!

Why did the skeleton go to the prom alone?
Because he couldn't find any body to go with.

TONGUE TWISTER

A big bug bit the little beetle but the little beetle bit the big bug back.

Knock Knock!
Who's there?
Beets!
Beets who?
Beets me!

Why are elephants so wrinkled?

Because they never do any ironing!

Can a kangaroo jump higher than the Statue of Liberty?
Of course! The Statue of Liberty can't jump!

Knock Knock!
Who's there?
Needle.
Needle who?
Needle little help with the door, it seems to be stuck.

 **Who's there?**
Maida.
Maida who?
Maida force be with you!

 **I can't eat this!**
Why not madam?
You haven't given me any cutlery.

 **Who's there?**
Double.
Double who?
W!

What type of birds never skip church on Sunday?
Birds of prey!

Who's there?
Bertha.
Bertha who?
Bertha-day greetings!

What kind of music do elves listen to?
Wrap!

Who's there?
Gladys.
Gladys who?
Gladys the weekend, I'm seeing my grandmother!

Knock Knock!

Why did the grasshopper go to the doctor?
Because he was feeling jumpy.

What do you get when you dip a kitten in chocolate?
A Kitty Kat!

 **I keep thinking I'm a spider.**
What a web of lies!

What did one flower say to the other flower?

Hey bud!

 **What did the mayonnaise say to the fridge?**
Close the door, I'm dressing!

Why are bananas never lonely?
Because they hang around in bunches.

 **Who's there?**
Clare.
Clare who?
Clare the way, I'm coming through!

What's better than having your hair in a bun?
Putting your teeth in a burger!

Knock Knock!

Who's there?
Turnip.
Turnip who?
Turnip the volume,
I can't hear the music!

Three is odd. Five is odd. But it's easy to make seven even. How? Just take off the 's'

What do you get when you cross a snake with pastry?
A pie-thon!

What do baby penguins sing when their Dad brings fish for dinner?
Freeze a Jolly Good Fellow!

Who's there?
Little old lady.
Little old lady who?
Wow! I didn't know you could yodel!

Who's there?
Alec!
Alec who?
Alec-tricity repair man.

What is yellow on the inside and green on the outside?
A banana dressed up as a cucumber!

What's black and white and makes an awful noise?
A zebra with a drum kit.

Student: I want to be an astronaut when I grow up.
Teacher: what high hopes you have!

What is a snake's favourite subject?
Hisssss-tory.

Knock Knock!
Who's there?
Annie.
Annie who?
Animals are about to eat me up, let me in!

Where do zombies go swimming?

In the Dead Sea!

Knock Knock!
Who's there?
Ooze.
Ooze who?
Ooze coming out to play?

Which cheese goes to church?

Holey cheese!

Why do parrots pass their exams?
Because they always suck seed.

What animal is no fun on April Fools' Day?
A snake, because you can't pull his leg!

What cheese is made backwards?
Edam!

Waiter, Waiter!

What is this fly doing in my soup?
Trying to swim to the side, sir.

 **Why was the man wearing trousers asked to leave the party?**
Because nobody had told him about the strict dress code.

How did the farmer mend the hole in his pants?
With a cabbage patch!

 **Who's there?**
Ammonia.
Ammonia who?
Ammonia man who's come to clean your toilet.

Knock Knock!

Who's there?
Lettuce.
Lettuce who?
Lettuce in, I've been here for hours!

Why did the fly fly?
Because the spider spied 'er!

Waiter, Waiter!

In future I'd like my soup without.
Without what, sir?
Without the chef's hair in it!

Who stole the soap?
The robber ducky.

What did the cute M&M say to the Mars Bar?
Are you going my Milky Way?

TONGUE TWISTER

Crisp crusts crackle crunchily.

Knock Knock!

Who's there?
Snow!
Snow who?
Snow school today – the heating is broken!

Any noise annoys an oyster but a noisy noise annoys an oyster more.

TONGUE TWISTER

Where do ants eat?
At a restaur-ant!

 **Who's there?**
Soup!
Soup who?
Superman!

**What do you get when you cross a robot
and a tractor?**
A transfarmer.

 **Why does it take pirates so long to
learn the alphabet?**
Because they spend years at C!

 **Will this lotion clear up my spots?**
I never make rash promises!

If you eat with your right hand but catch with your left, which one should you use to write?
Neither: use a pen!

 **What do you call eleven white birds on the ocean?**
Swan-sea United!

Our teacher went on a special banana diet.
Did she lose weight?
No, but she could climb trees really well!

 **Who's there?**
Thistle.
Thistle who?
Thistle be the last time I tell you about your broken doorbell!

What's green and gloopy and hangs from trees?

Giraffe snot!

Waiter, Waiter!

Why is my food a splodgy mess?
Well you did ask me to step on it, sir!

What do you call a man raking up leaves?
Russell!

If buttercups are yellow, what colour are hiccups?
Burple.

What kind of clothes does a clockmaker wear?
Second hand, of course!

How do you stop your pet bugs from flying away?
Be sure to zip up your flies!

Waiter, Waiter!

What on earth is this?
It's bean soup, sir.
I don't care what it was, what is it now?

What do you get if you cross a cement mixer with a chicken?
A brick-layer!

What do you call a smelly fairy?
Stinkerbell!

Where are teachers made?

On an assembly line!

 **Knock Knock!**

Who's there?
Canoe!
Canoe who?
Canoe come out and play
with me today?

**What's the best
way to stop
getting sick in the
winter?**

**Catch a
cold in the
summer.**

**What does Pooh Bear call
his girlfriend?**
Hunny!

**Why was the baby
ant confused?**
Because all his uncles were ants.

I'd tell you a joke about an umbrella, but it would go straight over your head.

Who's there?
Bean.
Bean who?
Bean knocking for 20 minutes!

If I tell you a joke about butter, will you promise not to spread it around?

There is a small slug in this lettuce.
I'm sorry madam,
did you want a bigger one?

I'd tell you a joke about a bed, but I haven't made it up yet.

What gives you the ability to walk through walls?
A door!

Knock Knock!

Who's there?
Watson.
Watson who?
What's on TV tonight?

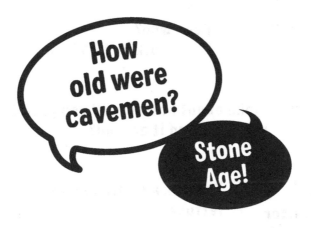

How old were cavemen?

Stone Age!

What word is always spelled wrong in the dictionary?
Wrong.

What is Dad's favourite Christmas carol?
Silent Night.

Knock Knock!

Who's there?
Snow.
Snow who?
Snowbody special!

What should you offer a fruit bowl in distress?
Lemon-aid!

What do you call a man with a seagull on his head?
Cliff!

What did the spider do on the computer?

Made a website!

She sells sea shells by the sea shore. The shells she sells are surely seashells. So if she sells shells on the seashore, I'm sure she sells seashore shells.

TONGUE TWISTER

What does a sea monster eat?
Fish and ships!

Who's there?
Juno.
Juno who?
Juno how to open this door?
It's stuck!

I think I'm a bell!
Sorry, I'm closed. I'll give you a ring in the morning.

Why did the iron stop working?
It ran out of steam.

What has four legs but can't walk?
A chair!

Knock Knock!

Who's there?
Celeste.
Celeste who?
Celeste time I'm telling you, open the door!

Where do spooks mail their letters?

At the ghost office!

What did Mickey say when Minnie asked him if he was listening?
I'm all ears!

How did the barber win the race?
He knew all the short cuts.

Why was the zombie so clever?
He had been eating a lot of Smarties!

 **Why are ghosts bad liars?**
Because you can see right through them!

What music are bubbles afraid of?
Pop music!

Why did the boy stare at the car radio?

He wanted to watch a car-tune!

If teachers want us to follow our dreams, why did I get extra homework for falling asleep?

Who's there?
Peas.
Peas who?
Peas let me in, I'm freezing!

Why did the farmer tiptoe around the farm?
He didn't want to wake the bulldozer!

Knock Knock!

Who's there?
Harmony!
Harmony who?
Harmony times do I have to tell you
to lock the door?

Why do stunt pilots often forget to put their pants on?

Because they've always got their head in the clouds!

Knock Knock!

Who's there?
Olaf!
Olaf who?
Olaf if you have to, but my pants have split!

Why was Cinderella rubbish at sport?
Because she was always running away from the ball!

Teacher: **Alex, spell horse.**
Alex: **H-O-R-S.**
Teacher: **But what's at the end of it?**
Alex: **A tail!**

Knock Knock!

Who's there?
Adore.
Adore who?
Adore can't stop me seeing you through the window, now open up!

Where do toads leave their jackets?

In the croakroom!

Did you hear what happened to the wooden car with a wooden engine and wooden wheels?
It wooden go!

TONGUE TWISTER

If two witches were watching two watches, which witch would watch which watch?

What did the bat say to his poorly friend as they flew past the cave?
Hang in there and you'll feel better soon!

Where does an elephant sit when he takes the train?
Anywhere he wants to!

What is the longest word in the world?
Smiles, because there is a mile between the first and last letters.

What do you call a sheep dipped in chocolate?
A Candy Baa.

Who's there?
Amy.
Amy who?
Amy 'fraid I've forgotten!

Now it's your turn!

Here are some awesome jokes sent in by 7-year-olds from around the world. Can you do better? See page 97!

Why does a cow go to the cinema?
To see a moooooovie!
(From Josie, Tunbridge Wells)

SENT IN BY
THOMAS, 7, FROM KENT

How did the magician cut the sea in half?
With a sea-saw! (From Thomas, Kent)

**What do you call a chicken
with lettuce in its eye?**
Chicken sees-a salad!
(From Alex, Peterborough)

Why did the banana go to hospital?
Because it wasn't peeling well!
(From Ciara, Lesmahagow)

**Why did the baker stop making
doughnuts?**
Because he was tired of the hole business!
(From Isla, Nova Scotia)

**What did the policeman say to his
tummy?**
Stop! You're under a vest!
(From Fenton, Kent)

Where do sheep go on holiday?
Baaaa-bados!
(From Oliver, Derby)

Mix and match!

Can you match each joke to its punchline? But watch out: there are two questions missing! You'll find them in **More Awesome Jokes Every 7 Year Old Should Know** – buy it now!

What's the meanest thing in the kitchen?

What do you call a dizzy pilot?

How does a comedian make omelettes?

What's the worst way to start keeping piranhas?

How does a cat make milkshakes?

How can you tell when a river is angry?

How does a mouse call his mum?

A pinch of salt!

Dip your toe in!

He'd forgotten to take his earwigs off!

He's a party pooper!

Using its whiskers!

She starts with a few wisecracks!

With a micro phone!

Flight headed!

Because it's foaming at the mouth!

How funny was that?

If you enjoyed the jokes in this book, I'm thrilled! (If not, please write your complaint on a fifty pound note and send to my address straight away).

If you're feeling kind, there's something really important you can do for me – tell other people that you enjoyed this book.

When a grown-up writes about it on Amazon, more people will see it... and that means I can carry on writing books for children. You just need to tell the big people what to say!

If you do write something nice, let me know – I promise I'll write back. My email address for jokes, notes and more is jokes@matwaugh.co.uk

I know a great joke!

Send me your best joke and I'll put it on my **World Map of Awesome Jokes**!

Head over to the map now to discover silly jokes, clever jokes and weird jokes. Some jokes rhyme, some are a crime, but they're all sent in by children like you!

Will you be the first on the map from your town?

Put your awesome joke here at
www.matwaugh.co.uk/jokemap

About Mat Waugh

It's funny what makes you laugh, isn't it? Sometimes it's a great joke, and I hope you found a few in this book. Sometimes you don't even need words. It could be a funny look from a friend in class. Or maybe it's something that wasn't supposed to happen.

Once, when I was about your age, I was in the back of my aunt's car on a Christmas Day. The sun reflected brightly in the deep puddles from the night's rain.

My aunt wasn't very good at driving. As we approached a dip in the road we could see a vicar cycling towards us, on his way to church. Dad told my aunt to slow down... but she pressed the wrong pedal. The car hit the water with a mighty SPLOOSH! I looked back to see a huge wave swamping the vicar and his bike. He shook his fists at us, but my aunt didn't even notice. I'm still laughing... but I bet the vicar isn't.

I have three daughters to make me laugh now. (Not all the time though: they drive me bananas.)

I live in Tunbridge Wells, which is a lively, lovely town in the south east of England. It's not a very funny place, mind you..

I've always written a lot. I've done lots of writing for other people – mostly serious stuff – but now I write silly, crazy and funny books as well.

Talking of crazy, I had a mad year when I thought I wanted to be a teacher. But then I found out how hard teachers work and that you have to buy your own biscuits. So now I just visit schools to eat their snacks and talk to children about stories.

Last thing: I love hearing from readers. Thoughts, jokes... anything. If that's you, then get in touch.

✉ mail@matwaugh.co.uk
www.matwaugh.co.uk

Or, if you're old enough:

f facebook.com/matwaughauthor
🐦 twitter.com/matwaugh

Three more to try!

Cheeky Charlie vol 1-6
Meet Harriet and her small, stinky brother. Together, they're trouble. Fabulously funny stories for kids aged 6 and up.

Fantastic Wordsearches
Wordsearch with a difference: themed, crossword clues and hidden words await!

The Fun Factor
When the fun starts vanishing, it seems Thora is the only one to notice. The headmaster is definitely up to no good, but what about Dad's new girlfriend? A mystery adventure for gadget-loving kids aged 8 and up.

Available from Amazon and local bookshops.

MORE
AWESOME JOKES
FOR 7 YEAR OLDS
OUT NOW!

Be the first to know about new stuff! Sign up for my emails at matwaugh.co.uk

---